Movable Feasts

The Outdoor and Self-Catering Recipe Book

by

Charlie Davis

Editions de la

Montagne

Published by

Editions de la
Montagne

PO Box 732
Southampton
SO16 7RQ
England

©2000 EdlM

ISBN 0 9533386 1 4

Origination by EdlM
Printed by IHDP

This book is dedicated to the many friends who have suffered my cooking on numerous expeditions

Thanks are also due to Adèle for her usual dedication and hard work and Marilyn for her appraisal and encouragement

"Loitering within tent
can ruin your cooking"
says Peg

and caravans are not much better - Ed.

He lied about the many friends - the garlic drove them away-Ed.

i

Foreword

w   The recipes are simple and straightforward since they are intended for easy and quick preparation with the minimum of fuss. Nevertheless, they are anything but boring!

w   Most of the ingredients are readily available but don't worry if you haven't all that is required for a particular dish. Substitute! You'll be amazed what a little imagination can do!

w   The main intention of this book is to show what can be achieved with a pan or two, one or two burners, maybe a barbecue or grill and certainly some ingenuity, although obviously, all campers, caravanners and sailors have different equipment, differing requirements and tastes.

w   Quantities are not critical and are volumetric rather than weight-based to avoid the need for weighing. Scales are for lounge lizards not adventurers!

w   Increase / decrease quantities according to the number of lucky diners or their appetites!

w   All peelable items apart from potatoes in jackets are assumed to be peeled! Similarly, cans and packets are to be opened, pips and stones to be removed and vegetables to be washed! Need I say more?

w   If you don't like cooking with wine, drink it instead - it will improve the meal no end!

w   Garlic isn't compulsory! - but remember the Mediterranean adage: "He who has eaten garlic cannot tell whether his companion has."
(and it keeps away werewolves - handy if in a tent!)

Enjoy your meal!!

Contents

Symbols

Ingredients

Method

Approximate cooking time   e.g. 15 mins   1 hour

Utensils

Pan as available - frying pan, saucepan, mess tin

Number of burners

Number of people

Barbecue

Grill

Bowl / heatproof dish

Additional pot and burner for rice etc if available

The bare minimum of utensils and heat sources is given. If you have more, use
them if you want!

Avocado Stick

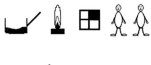

2 knobs butter / tablespoons oil
1 large, ripe avocado
3 or 4 rashers of bacon or slices of cold meat or sausage
1 small onion
1 clove of garlic
1 large tomato
6 medium mushrooms
1 fresh French stick
salt and pepper

Chop the vegetables and meat into small pieces and fry until cooked. Season if required. Meanwhile, peel the avocado and remove the stone. Mash with a crushed clove of garlic if desired, mix with the cooked meat and vegetables and heap into the split stick. The filling can be used cold too.

Bacon Kebabs with Savoury Rice

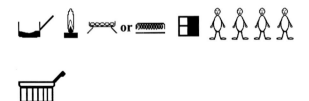

8 rashers bacon cut in half
1 can cocktail sausages
1 dozen or so button mushrooms
1 small can pineapple chunks
olive oil
2 mugs long grained rice
1 onion finely chopped
2 knobs butter
stock cubes

Savoury rice: Fry onion and rice over moderate heat until rice is
golden. Add 2 mugs stock, bring to the boil and simmer until water
is absorbed and rice is tender - about 20 minutes. Wrap bacon
around sausages and thread alternately on skewers with pineapple
and mushrooms. Brush with oil and grill or barbecue gently for
about 7 minutes. Time the cooking so that rice and kebabs are
ready at the same time.

Bacon Ratatouille

8 rashers streaky bacon cut into strips
1 tablespoon oil
1 aubergine sliced
1 green pepper sliced
2 medium onions sliced
1 clove garlic crushed
6-8 mushrooms
1 can tomatoes
salt and pepper to taste

Fry bacon and put aside. Fry green pepper, aubergine, onion until soft. Add bacon, tomatoes, garlic and seasoning. Cook gently for 10 minutes. Eat with plain boiled rice and green salad.

Barbecued Chicken

8 chicken pieces, several cloves of garlic - some crushed, some sliced
3-4 tablespoons lemon juice
2 teaspoons ground ginger
½ mug cooking oil
2 tablespoons sesame seeds
¼ mug soy sauce

Slit skin of chicken and insert slivers of garlic. Put meat in pan, mix other ingredients and pour over. Leave to marinate for at least 30 minutes. Wrap each piece of chicken separately in kitchen foil after adding a tablespoon of marinade to each. Grill until done. Unwrap and add more marinade before sprinkling with sesame seeds and cooking until seeds have turned golden. Discard marinade which has been in contact with raw chicken.

Barbecued Tandoori Chicken

4 large or 8 small chicken portions
3-4 tablespoons lemon juice
1 teaspoon salt
1 onion chopped
1 carton plain yogourt
2 cloves garlic chopped or crushed
1 teaspoon ground ginger
2-3 teaspoons tandoori spice or curry powder if tandoori is not to hand

Mix marinade ingredients and pour over chicken, ensuring it is all covered. Leave to marinate as long as possible - overnight if you can. Barbecue for 20-25 minutes, bone side down, turn over and cook for another 10-15 minutes until done. Eat with baked potatoes in their jackets and salad.

Beansprout and Kidney Bean Salad

1 small can beansprouts
1 small can kidney beans
½ mug sliced mushrooms
1 red pepper sliced
6 spring onions chopped

dressing number 3 on page 72

Make the dressing. Pour dressing over salad and turn thoroughly. Any excess can be used as a marinade and sauce for barbecuing or grilling meat.

Substitutes: Butterbeans, cooked chicory, broccoli or cauliflower.

Beef Baguette

2 knobs butter / tablespoons oil
1 medium onion
6 medium mushrooms
garlic if wished
1 small pack of minced beef
1 fresh French stick
salt and pepper
1 tablespoonful of curry powder

Put half the oil / butter in the pan to heat. Add curry powder to beef and stir well. Fry until done (about 3-4 minutes). Put aside, then roughly chop the vegetables and cook until tender - about 5 minutes. Mix beef into vegetables and reheat for a few moments. Season to taste. Split and fill the fresh French stick with the cooked vegetable and meat mixture.

Beefburger Hongrois

1 pack of minced beef
1 onion finely chopped

Sauce

2 knobs butter
2 onions sliced
1 handful button mushrooms sliced
2 tablespoons flour
2 tablespoons paprika
1 can tomatoes
2 dessert spoons tomato paste
1 tablespoon lemon juice
1 mug stock, salt and pepper
4 tablespoons soured cream

Mix meat, seasoning and onion. Divide and flatten into burgers.
Grill or barbecue. Make sauce in pan by frying onions and mushrooms in butter then adding flour and frying for 1 - 2 minutes
more. Add remaining ingredients except cream and simmer for 5
minutes. Stir cream into sauce just before serving with burgers.

Bean Bubble and Squeak

cold mashed potato
cold chopped cabbage
any other leftover vegetables plus baked beans
1 small onion sliced
2 rashers cooked bacon, chopped
2 tablespoons oil
seasoning

Roughly mash the vegetables and bacon together. Spread into a
flat, thick 'pancake' and fry over medium heat until brown on both
sides.

*"Old motorcaravanners don't change their ideas - they just
stick in the mud"*

Beetroot Salad

1 medium beetroot cooked and diced
2 sticks celery chopped
salad dressing number 4 on page 72

Carrot and Courgette Salad

1 large carrot grated
1 courgette grated
1 onion chopped
plus salad dressing 1 on page 72

Mix all ingredients thoroughly in either recipe.

Cheese and Tomato Soup

1 small onion finely chopped
1 knob of butter
1 tablespoon of flour
1½ mugs vegetarian stock or water
2 mugs milk
2 large chopped tomatoes
1 mug of finely chopped Cheddar cheese
salt and pepper to taste

Fry onion in saucepan until soft. Add flour and cook slowly for 2 minutes. Gradually blend in stock or water, and cook until soup comes to boil and thickens slightly, stirring all the time. Add tomatoes and seasoning. Cover pan and simmer for 10 - 15 minutes then add the milk and bring up to temperature. Remove from heat and stir in cheese until it melts.

Cheesy Chips

2 large potatoes cut into thick chips
2 large slices of Cheddar or similar
2-3 tablespoons oil
2 teaspoons mixed herbs
salt and pepper
2 tablespoons soy sauce
2 cloves garlic chopped finely
aluminium foil

Divide the potato into 2 piles. Place each on a sheet of foil cut to
size and season. Add oil, wrap and cook under the grill or on a
barbecue until done - about 20 minutes or so, depending on the
heat available. Unwrap carefully and add cheese, soy sauce,
garlic and herbs. Cook unwrapped on the foil for a further 5
minutes until cheese has melted.

Chicken and Turkey Glazes / Marinades

These can be used to coat poultry before and during cooking to give a variety of different flavours.

Chilli, Mango and Garlic

Mix 2 teaspoons hot chilli sauce with 4 tablespoons mango chutney and 1 clove crushed garlic.

Ginger and orange

Mix 1 tablespoon soy sauce with ½ teaspoon ground ginger and 3 tablespoons marmalade.

Sweet and Sour

Mix 3 tablespoons honey with 1 tablespoon tomato paste, 1 tablespoon soy sauce, 2 teaspoons Worcestershire sauce and 2 teaspoons plum sauce if available.

Groundnut and Garlic

Mix 4 tablespoons crunchy peanut butter with 1-2 teaspoons oil and crushed garlic.

Honey and lemon

Mix 3 tablespoons honey with crushed garlic and 2 teaspoons lemon juice.

Garlic and Tomato

Mix 4 crushed cloves of garlic with 2 tablespoons soy sauce, ½ teaspoon black pepper and 2 tablespoons tomato paste.

Mustard and Chilli

Mix 2 teaspoons mustard powder with 1 tablespoon oil, a pinch of salt and pepper, 1 tablespoon Worcestershire sauce and ½ teaspoon chilli powder.

Soy, garlic and chilli

Mix 6 tablespoons dark soy sauce, 2 cloves crushed garlic, ½ teaspoon chilli powder.

Curry and lemon

Mix 2 level teaspoons curry powder with two tablespoons oil and 3 teaspoons lemon juice.

Peanut and curry

Mix 4 tablespoons crunchy peanut butter with 1-2 teaspoons oil and 1 tablespoon curry powder.

Honey, Soy and Tomato

Mix 3 tablespoons honey with 2 tablespoons dark soy sauce and 2 tablespoons tomato paste.

Tomato, Pesto and Ginger

Mix 3 tablespoons tomato paste with 1 tablespoon pesto and 1 teaspoon prepared ginger paste or ground ginger.

Blackberry, crab apple and ginger

Boil a handful of blackberries and a few crab apples from a late Summer hedgerow in a little water. Add a teaspoon of ginger. Wonderful with pork!

Chicken Curry

4 chicken joints
4 tablespoons flour
2 knobs butter
1 tablespoon oil
2 large onions chopped, 1 large cooking apple chopped
1 clove garlic chopped
1 tablespoon curry powder
1 teaspoon ground ginger, ½ teaspoon cinnamon
1 teaspoon salt
1 tablespoon chutney
½ mug milk, ½ mug water
1 small carton plain yogourt
accompaniments: peanuts, chopped fresh tomatoes, plain boiled
rice

Fry floured chicken until golden and remove to plate. Fry onions,
apple, and garlic until pale gold. Stir in salt, curry powder, spices,
chutney, milk and water. Add chicken and bring to boil. Cover and
cook for ¾ to 1 hour until meat is tender. Stir in yogourt and heat
without boiling for further 5 minutes. Eat with accompaniments.

Chicken in White Sauce

2 chicken breasts cubed
2 onions chopped
2 tablespoons flour
2 knobs butter
½ mug milk
mixed herbs
chicken stock cube
1 teaspoon ground ginger
1 teaspoon lemon juice
a clove of garlic crushed

Fry chicken slowly in butter until golden then remove from heat.
Fry onions, add flour and cook for a couple of minutes, then
slowly add milk and the crumbled stock cube, stirring all the time.
Add remainder of ingredients and simmer till thick. Put chicken
back in pan and heat through. Season to taste. Eat with your
choice of accompaniments such as plain baked potato and green
salad.

Chicken Satay

6-8 chicken breasts cubed

Marinade:
2 teaspoons ground coriander
2 tablespoons soy sauce
1 teaspoon turmeric
1 teaspoon cumin
2 tablespoons lime juice
2 tablespoons oil

Sauce:
2 tablespoons oil
1 onion chopped
1 teaspoon chilli powder
½ mug peanut butter
1 teaspoon brown sugar

Mix marinade in deepish pot and marinate meat for as long as possible. Thread meat on skewers and grill, basting frequently with oil. Cook onion with chilli powder in the oil, combine with peanut butter and sugar to make the sauce and use to brush meat for the final 2 minutes of cooking.

Chicken Stew

4 chicken breasts chopped into bite-sized pieces
3 tablespoons olive oil
1 large onion chopped
3 cloves garlic chopped
2 teaspoons chilli powder
1 tablespoon ground cumin
1 tablespoon ground coriander
2 cans chopped tomatoes
2 tablespoons tomato purée
3-4 tablespoons ground almonds
4 tablespoons chocolate pieces (plain or milk)
fresh coriander
1 bunch spring onions, seasoning

Fry chicken for 5 minutes, turning occasionally. Remove from pan
and fry onion. Then stir in chilli, garlic, cumin, ground coriander
and cook for 30 seconds. Put in remainder of ingredients apart
from chocolate and fresh coriander. Add chicken, cover and cook
for 30 minutes. Stir in chocolate until melted and add fresh
coriander. Eat with rice and chopped spring onions.

Chicory Salad

4 rashers streaky bacon
1 head of chicory
2 sticks celery
1 small can of sweetcorn drained
a handful of salted peanuts
2 slices ham chopped
½ carton of natural yogourt
1 teaspoonful of lemon juice if available
salt and pepper

Chop and cook bacon. Put aside. Pierce can of corn in two places and upend to drain. Cut chicory into rings and chop celery. Add corn, peanuts, bacon and ham. Mix in the yogourt and lemon juice just before eating. Season to taste.

Chilli Con Carne

1 can red kidney or haricot beans
2 medium onions and 2 cloves garlic
1 small pack of minced lean beef
2 knobs butter and 2 teaspoons olive or corn oil
1 can tomatoes
1 green pepper
1 teaspoon chilli powder
1 pinch of salt, 1 teaspoon caraway seeds
½ mug water
1 tablespoon flour
4 tablespoons top of the milk or single cream if available

Drain beans by piercing two holes in top of can. Fry chopped
onion and garlic in butter and oil until golden. Add meat and fry
for 5 minutes, breaking up with a fork and stirring until mixed and
evenly fried. Add chopped tomatoes, deseeded and chopped
pepper, beans, chilli powder, salt, caraway seeds, and half the
water. Cover and cook over very low heat for ¾ hour or until
beans are soft. Stir occasionally. Mix flour with rest of water, add
to pan, cook until mixture thickens, remove from heat, and stir in
cream.

Chinese Fried Pork

about 3 mugs of diced pork
1 tablespoon soy sauce
1 teaspoon salt
1 teaspoon brown sugar
1 tablespoon white wine
1 tablespoon flour
3 knobs butter
1 chopped onion
8-10 medium mushrooms
2 large tomatoes skinned and chopped
4 tablespoons cooked or frozen peas

Stir pork in soy sauce, salt, wine, sugar and flour mixture until coated. Fry onion until golden and put aside. Fry pork until browned, then add other vegetables including onion and cook gently for another 10 minutes, stirring frequently. Eat with rice.

Chopped Pork and Ham Grill

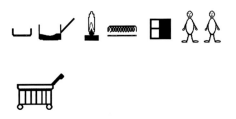

1 handful of quick macaroni
1 medium onion sliced
1 knob of butter
2 tablespoons of flour
1 cup of milk
1 tablespoon of tomato purée
1 can of luncheon meat
½ cup of grated Cheddar or similar hard cheese
2 sliced tomatoes
salt and pepper

Cook macaroni in boiling salted water for 8 minutes or as directed on pack. Fry onions in half the butter until soft and add drained macaroni. Put remaining butter, flour, and milk in pan and heat, whisking continuously until sauce is thick. Stir in purée and seasoning. Dice meat, stir into macaroni and onions with the sauce and half the cheese. Put into a flat dish, arrange tomatoes on top of mixture and sprinkle with rest of cheese. Grill for 25 minutes.

Confused Eggs

6 medium eggs
2 tablespoons double cream
1 knob butter
1 teaspoon chopped parsley
2 rashers smoked bacon lightly cooked
seasoning

Beat eggs with seasoning and cream. Grill or fry bacon and cut into strips. Melt butter in pan and pour in eggs. Stir continuously until cooked then stir in bacon and parsley. Serve on toast or lightly fried bread if no grill is available.

Peg says "Old guys may give way under the strain"

Coq au Vin

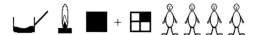

4 chicken joints
4 tablespoons flour
1 teaspoon salt
2 knobs butter
1 tablespoon oil
1 large onion chopped
1 clove garlic chopped
1 mug lean chopped bacon
8 small onions or shallots
2 teaspoons chopped parsley
1 bay leaf
1 mug red wine
4 tablespoons water
8 or so medium mushrooms sliced

Toss chicken in seasoned flour, fry until golden in saucepan.
Remove and put aside. Add chopped onion, garlic and bacon to
remaining oil in pan, frying until just turned colour. Put chicken
back, add rest of ingredients apart from mushrooms. Boil and
lower heat, cover and simmer for an hour, add the mushrooms and
simmer for a further 15 minutes.

Curried Chicken Hotpot

4 chicken pieces
4 tablespoons oil
2 cloves garlic peeled and chopped finely
curry powder
1 leek cut into rings
1 onion sliced
1 stick celery chopped
1 green pepper seeded and sliced
2-3 chicken stock cubes
2 mugs long grained rice
2 tablespoons flour

Fry the chicken for a few minutes until browned. Sprinkle with flour and continue to cook for a further 5 minutes. Mix chicken stock in a mug of hot water and pour over chicken. Add vegetables and curry powder to taste. Cover and cook for ¾ hour. Serve with rice.

Curry Sauce

2 knobs butter
2 teaspoons oil
2 large onions finely chopped
1 clove garlic finely chopped
2 tablespoons curry powder
1 tablespoon flour
1 tablespoon tomato paste
2 tablespoons chutney or sweet pickle
1 tablespoon lemon juice
3 teaspoons sugar
1½ mugs stock or water
ground ginger and cinnamon if available
salt to taste

Fry onion and garlic in oil and butter until soft. Stir in curry powder and flour and add tomato paste, chutney, lemon juice, sugar and also ginger and cinnamon if used. Blend in stock or water, add salt, bring to boil and then simmer for ¾ hour. Can be used with cooked meat, poultry, fish, eggs or vegetables.

Devilled Pork Sausages

1 pack pork sausages
1 large knob of butter
1 medium sized onion chopped
2 tablespoons flour
¾ mug of water
2 teaspoons Worcestershire sauce
1 teaspoon made mustard
2 tablespoons sweet pickle
2 tablespoons tomato ketchup
1 tablespoon vinegar

Fry sausages in butter until brown and remove from pan. Add onion and fry gently until golden. Stir in the flour and cook for 1 minute. Add remaining ingredients and slowly bring to boil, stirring. Return sausages to pan, lower heat, add lid and simmer until sausages are cooked.

Fish with Orange

4 thin white fish fillets
4 tablespoons orange marmalade
1 knob butter
2 tablespoons orange juice
salt and pepper

Cut fillets lengthwise and coat with marmalade. Heat butter and orange juice in pan and season. Add fish fillets and cook for about 8 minutes. Serve with a vegetable such as carrots if a second burner is available, or a salad.

"I may be an old guy but I know the ropes"

Fish with Pesto Sauce

2 white fish fillets
2 tablespoons white wine
2 tablespoons prepared pesto sauce
4 tablespoons fromage frais
fresh basil

Bring wine to boil, reduce heat and add fish, cover and simmer for 5 minutes. Mix pesto and fromage frais, add to fish, heat and stir gently for 2-3 minutes. Garnish with basil and serve with pasta.

"Old campers don't peg out any more.

They caravan instead"

Garlic Bread

1 or 2 baguettes
2 cloves garlic
4 knobs butter
salt and pepper
parsley chopped
rosemary chopped

Cut the loaf almost through in thick slices. Mix the peeled, crushed garlic with the herbs, salt and pepper and blend with the softened butter. Spread between the cuts in the French stick and wrap in a sheet of buttered aluminium foil. Heat on the embers for 20 minutes per side or similar under a grill.

Glazed Chicken

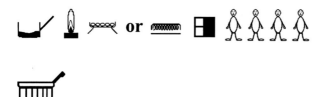

2 tablespoons clear honey
2 tablespoons soy sauce
1 tablespoon white wine vinegar
8 chicken drumsticks or small pieces, fresh or defrosted

Heat honey, soy sauce and vinegar gently in a pan. Cut slits in chicken and brush with mixture. Cook for 15-20 minutes, turning and brushing occasionally with mixture.

"I always go on holiday with several guys" says Peg!

Grilled Fresh Sardines

several sardines according to size
fresh chopped basil
1 teaspoon rosemary
2 tablespoons lemon juice
1 teaspoon ground ginger
olive oil
salt and pepper
aluminium foil

Behead and gut the fish. Clean out the insides with the edge of a
knife, wash in salted water, drain and shake dry. Oil, salt and
pepper the fish, sprinkle with the chopped herbs, lemon juice and
ginger and wrap in foil. Pierce several small holes in the bottom of
the foil and put the parcels on the coals or under the grill for 10-20
minutes depending on size and the heat available. Check once or
twice to see if the fish is done. Eat with a green salad or similar.

Grilled Gammon

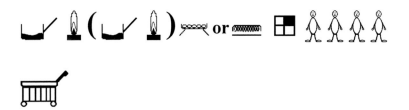

4 thick gammon rashers
3 knobs butter (1 melted)
2 teaspoons tomato purée
¼ teaspoon sugar
¼ teaspoon Worcestershire sauce

Remove gammon rinds and snip fat at intervals to avoid curling. Brush with 1 knob melted butter and grill or barbecue for 5-7 minutes or until fat turns clear. Turn over and do the same to the other side. Meanwhile, cream the other 2 knobs of butter (NOT that used to brush the raw gammon!) with purée, Worcestershire sauce and sugar. When meat is cooked, use to top each rasher. Eat with barbecued potatoes, rice or noodles.

Grilled Potato Slices

2 large potatoes sliced about ½ inch (12mm) thick
3 tablespoons oil
salt and pepper

Brush slices with oil, season and grill both sides until brown and tender.

They can also be wiped with garlic or coated with one of the glazes described on pages 13-14.

See also Cheesy Chips on Page 12

Grilled Zucchini

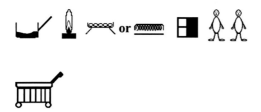

4 courgettes
4 tablespoons tomato paste
4 tablespoons grated Parmesan cheese
2 tablespoons Worcestershire sauce
4 cloves garlic crushed
2 tablespoons olive oil
salt and pepper

Boil courgettes in salted water for 3-4 minutes, halve lengthways, coat with oil and put flat side down on barbecue or up if using a grill. Cook for 4-5 minutes. Mix remainder of ingredients apart from oil and spread over flat side of courgettes. Continue cooking for 5-10 minutes until tender. Use as an accompaniment for grilled meats.

Ham and Coleslaw Salad

1 piece white cabbage shredded
2 dessert apples grated
1 large carrot grated
1 heaped tablespoon raisins
1 small onion finely chopped
1 orange
1 carton of natural yogourt
1 tablespoon mayonnaise
1 teaspoon lemon juice
2 or 3 slices of ham
seasoning

Mix cabbage, apple, carrot, finely grated orange rind, raisins and
onions with half the juice from the orange. Stir in yogourt,
mayonnaise, lemon juice, salt and pepper. Garnish with orange
slices and serve with ham. (Tuna is a good alternative).

Hawaian Tuna

1 medium can of tuna flaked
1 medium can of pineapple
3 leeks finely sliced
1 mug stock
1 tablespoon cornflour
1 tablespoon brown sugar
1 tablespoon vinegar
poppy seeds or nuts if available
pack of noodles

Simmer leeks for 3 minutes in stock, add pineapple fruit and juice.
Mix cornflour, sugar and vinegar and stir into boiling stock
mixture. Continue stirring until thick and clear. Add the tuna and
cook for further 2 minutes. Eat with noodles sprinkled with poppy
seeds or nuts.

Hot Chicken Pieces

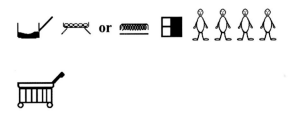

1 tablespoon cayenne pepper
8 tablespoons lemon juice
1 teaspoon mustard powder
1 onion finely chopped
2 tablespoons Worcestershire sauce
salt and ground black pepper
8 chicken drumsticks or small pieces, fresh or defrosted

Mix marinade ingredients and pour over chicken pieces. Stir to coat. Leave for as long as possible - 2 or 3 hours if you can. Preheat grill or barbecue. Cook for 15-20 minutes, turning and brushing with the marinade frequently. Serve hot or cold with salad.

Hot Sardine Toast Starter

2 cans sardines in oil
2 slices of bread
1 teaspoon chilli sauce
1 clove of garlic crushed
1 teaspoon lemon juice

Toast the bread, more on one side than the other. Drain the sardines, open them up so that they are flat and wipe with crushed garlic, lemon juice and chilli. Arrange fish on the less toasted side of bread, place under grill and heat for a minute or two, ensuring that the toast does not burn.

Hot Sausage Crisps

1 pack sausages
1 large egg
2 teaspoons milk
4 tablespoons breadcrumbs toasted in the pan beforehand
2 teaspoons dry mustard
salt and pepper
a deepish pan of hot oil (a couple of inches / 5 cm is adequate)

Cut each sausage into 4 pieces. Beat egg and milk well. Combine breadcrumbs, mustard, salt and pepper. Coat sausages with egg mixture and roll in breadcrumbs. Fry until crisp and golden.

Variation: Beef balls - minced beef rolled and coated as above or with chopped salted peanuts.

Jacket Potatoes

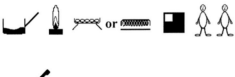

2 large scrubbed potatoes (use a pan scrubber!)
1 mug of chopped or grated cheese
1 can of baked beans
2 rashers streaky bacon
2 eggs

Boil potatoes for 10-15 minutes until softened through, cut lengthways, hollow out some of the centre, crack egg into hollow, place
on barbecue or under grill and heat until egg is done. Meanwhile
mix the grated cheese with the beans and heat. Grill the bacon.
Serve with salad.

Alternative fillings for baked potatoes:

Blue Cheese and Mayonnaise

Crumble a chunk of blue cheese such as Danish Blue, add 4
tablespoons mayonnaise and stir in a little chopped onion and
garlic. Season.

Fried Onion, Bacon and Mushroom

Fry chopped ingredients in a little oil. Fill split potato and top with grated Cheddar cheese.

Avocado and Salmon

Cream the avocado flesh with salt and pepper to taste. Flake the canned salmon and mix gently into the avocado.

Shrimp and Mayonnaise

Drain a small can of shrimps, mix with 4 tablespoons mayonnaise, add a teaspoon of lemon juice, season with salt and pepper. Add chopped spring onions.

Fried Tomato, Onion and Basil

Fry chopped tomato and onion until soft and add chopped basil.

Tuna and Mayonnaise

Flake drained tuna into mayonnaise and season.

Try also:

Grilled / Fried chopped fish fingers and tartare sauce

Garlic Butter and chopped peanuts

Curried baked beans

Chopped celery, grated Cheddar and finely chopped onion

Avocado, Shrimp and Spring Onion

Avocado and Sardine

Leek, Orange and Celery Salad

1 large leek cut into rings
2 sticks celery chopped or a mugful of chopped celeriac
2 tablespoons prepared pesto
2 tablespoons Parmesan cheese grated
4 tablespoons yogourt
1 small orange segmented
seasoning

Season and mix all ingredients.

Variations:

Add 4 slices chopped ham

or ½ can sweetcorn

or ½ can cold baked beans

or 1 mug cold diced potato

Lettuce and Parmesan Salad

1 lettuce chopped
2 tablespoons grated Parmesan cheese
3 tablespoons mayonnaise
2 tablespoons fromage frais
2 cloves garlic crushed, 2 tomatoes chopped
1 small onion sliced
salt and pepper

 Mix all ingredients in a bowl until thoroughly coated

Pasta Salad

2 mugs cold cooked pasta to replace lettuce in recipe above.

Mexican Cod

2 cod steaks
2 knobs butter
oil
1 red and 1 green pepper deseeded and chopped
1 tablespoon cornflour
1 can tomatoes
a handful of sweet corn
salt and pepper
rice for 2 people

Brush steaks with oil, season and grill or barbecue for about 15 minutes or until cooked. Fry peppers in the butter. Blend in the cornflour and cook for 2-3 minutes. Add tomatoes, corn and seasoning and simmer for 5 minutes. Eat the steaks on a bed of boiled rice with the sauce poured over.

Minestrone Soup

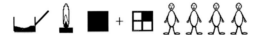

1 leek trimmed and shredded
1 handful of chopped green beans
1 large onion finely sliced
1 carrot finely sliced
2 stalks celery chopped small
½ small cabbage cut into thin strips
1 can tomatoes
a few haricot beans soaked overnight or canned
2 tablespoons chopped parsley
1 teaspoon chopped basil
2 teaspoons salt
ground black pepper
1 teaspoon sugar
3 mugs water
1 small handful broken macaroni or spaghetti
1 mug grated Cheddar or Parmesan cheese

Put the vegetables in a pan with the water, seasoning and sugar.
Bring to the boil, lower heat, simmer for 1 hour adding more water
as necessary, then add pasta, simmering for another 15 minutes.
Eat sprinkled with cheese.

Mushroom and Lentil Soup

about 20 button mushrooms sliced
1 onion chopped
1 clove garlic crushed
2 carrots grated
1 tablespoon oil
2 tablespoons water
2 mugs stock
¾ mug red lentils
4 or 5 dried apricots chopped
½ teaspoon coriander ground
2 teaspoons grated orange peel
juice of 1 orange
4 tablespoons natural yogourt
salt and pepper

Cook onion, garlic, carrot for 5 minutes in the oil and water. Add
stock and all ingredients except mushrooms and orange juice.
Cook for 20 minutes, add mushrooms and juice and more water if
necessary. Simmer for a further 2 minutes. Serve with swirl of
yogourt and sprinkling of herbs.

Mushroom and Turkey Stroganoff

1 large knob butter
2 tablespoons olive oil or vegetable oil
4 turkey breasts
1 onion thinly sliced
a dozen or so mixed varieties of mushrooms roughly chopped
3 tablespoons apple juice or brandy
1 tablespoon flour
½ teaspoon paprika
1 small pot crème fraîche
1 mug chicken stock
1 tablespoon tomato paste
1 tablespoon chopped parsley

Heat half the butter and half the oil. Season breasts and fry
quickly until brown. Remove. Heat remaining oil and butter in pan
and fry onion and mushrooms for 3-4 minutes. Add apple juice or
brandy and reduce slightly. Stir in flour and paprika and cook for
further 1-2 minutes. Add crème fraîche, stock and tomato paste,
season and bring to boil, stirring continuously for further 1-2
minutes. reduce heat, add breasts and cook gently stirring
occasionally for 8-10 minutes. Stir in parsley. Serve with rice and
lightly cooked courgettes.

Mushroom Sauce

A handful of mushrooms finely chopped
2 mugs of milk
1 stick of celery diced
1 bayleaf, 2 whole cloves
2 knobs butter
2 tablespoons flour
1 teaspoon lemon juice
2 tablespoons double cream
salt and pepper

Put celery, onion, bayleaf, salt, pepper and milk in a pan and bring
to boil. Cool and strain into a jug or other pan. Fry mushrooms in
butter for 2-3 minutes, add flour, stirring well. Remove from heat
and stir in milk. Bring to boil and stir until sauce thickens. Simmer
for 2 minutes, stir in lemon juice and cream. Serve hot with meat,
fish or vegetables.

Neapolitan Spaghetti

sufficient spaghetti for 4 people (see pack)
2 knobs butter
2 teaspoons olive oil
1 onion sliced
1 clove garlic crushed
2 slices ham chopped or 4 rashers bacon chopped and fried
2 tablespoons flour
6 chopped tomatoes
1 tablespoon tomato purée
1 mug stock
1 bay leaf, 1 blade mace or teaspoon ground mace
6 white peppercorns
1 teaspoon brown sugar
2 teaspoons lemon juice
salt and pepper, fresh basil chopped

Fry onion, bacon or ham and garlic until golden. Stir in flour, tomatoes, purée, stock, bay leaf, mace, peppercorns, basil and sugar. Bring to boil, reduce heat, cover and simmer for 45 minutes. Add lemon juice and season. Put spaghetti on to boil in salted water some 15 minutes before end of cooking time for sauce.

Noodle Supper

1 pack of cocktail sausages
1 large onion finely chopped
1 clove garlic crushed
1 tablespoon oil
3 celery sticks chopped
½ red and ½ green pepper sliced
2 dozen or so button mushrooms sliced
1 mug of dry cider
2 teaspoons demerara sugar
noodles or tagliatelle sufficient for 4 people (see pack)
2 tablespoons mixed herbs (preferably fresh)

Grill or barbecue sausages for 5-6 minutes on each side or until cooked and then put aside. Fry onion and garlic until soft. Add celery, peppers, mushrooms, sausages, cider and sugar. Bring to boil and simmer for 15 minutes, stirring occasionally. Cook pasta for about 10 minutes until *al dente*, i.e. you can just squeeze between fingernails or it is firm to the bite, not too soft or hard. Stir herbs into the mixture and pour over drained pasta. Stir and serve with the sausages.

Orange and Watercress Salad

1 bunch watercress
1 large orange
1 medium onion cut into thin rings or a few chopped spring onions
2 tablespoons olive oil
salt and pepper

Thoroughly wash the watercress, break into sprigs and put in a bowl. Peel the orange, discard the pith, divide fruit into segments over the bowl so that any juice is caught. Add the orange to the watercress, together with the onion. Mix the oil and orange juice with salt and pepper to taste and pour over the salad. Toss.

"Swinging guys can let you down"

Parmesan Pasta

sufficient tagliatelle for 4 people (see packet)
2 mugs of frozen peas thawed
4 slices ham cut into strips
2 tablespoons olive oil
2 tablespoons grated Parmesan cheese
2 teaspoons Italian seasoning
garlic if wished

For a vegetarian alternative: replace ham with chopped
walnuts or other nuts and add broccoli florets to the peas.

Put pasta in boiling water and return to boil. Simmer for 8
minutes. Add peas for the last 5 minutes. Drain and add other
ingredients. Stir well and heat through.

Pasta, Mushroom and Ham Salad

a handful of mushrooms sliced
2 mugs of pasta shapes such as conchiglie, farfalle or spirali
½ cucumber cut into matchsticks
4 large tomatoes peeled and sliced
4 slices ham in strips
2 tablespoons sunflower oil
1 teaspoon vinegar
1 teaspoon oregano
salt and pepper

Cook pasta according to instructions, drain and cool. Mix pasta, cucumber, ham, mushrooms and tomatoes. Whisk other ingredients together then pour over pasta and mix. If possible cool before serving.

Pasta with Spicy Sausage

1 large onion and 1 large red chilli finely chopped
3 tablespoons flour
2 tablespoons olive oil
2 cloves garlic crushed
2 cans plum tomatoes
1 tablespoon sugar
1 pack of spicy sausages
1 pack of pasta (e.g. twists)
salt and pepper

Season flour with salt and pepper, fry onion, chilli and garlic for 4-5 minutes until soft and lightly coloured. Drain tomatoes, add with the sugar to the onion and simmer for 30 minutes or until reduced by half. Skin the sausages, shape the meat into walnut sized balls and roll in seasoned flour. Fry in remaining oil until golden brown (2-3 minutes). Add to tomato sauce and simmer for 15 minutes. Meanwhile cook the pasta until *al dente* (just tender). Drain and add to sauce. Season to taste and stir.

Peanut Coleslaw

½ small white cabbage shredded
2 celery sticks chopped
1 small dessert apple, cored and thinly sliced
1 tablespoon natural yogourt
3 tablespoons mayonnaise
4 spring onions chopped
2 tablespoons chopped parsley
a handful of salted roast peanuts
salt and pepper

Mix all ingredients in a bowl or pan until cabbage is thoroughly coated.

Variations:

Grated carrot, chopped fried tomato and onion, fried mushroom and onion, chopped avocado.

Pepper and Cheese Boats

2 yellow or red peppers sliced lengthways, deseeded and the
stalks removed
a mug of grated cheese such as Cheddar
a clove of garlic finely chopped
a few roast salted peanuts
Worcestershire sauce

Eat with barbecued / grilled chops, burgers, chicken, or as a
starter.

Lightly grill or barbecue the peppers with the open side up for a
few minutes, then fill with a mixture of chopped garlic, cheese,
nuts and a dash of Worcestershire sauce and grill until the cheese
melts.

Fillings can be varied according to what you have available and
what, if anything, you are going to eat with them:

For example:

Baked beans with curry powder stirred in and fried onion topping.

Chopped grilled or barbecued bacon with baked beans.

Scrambled egg and chopped grilled sausage.

Hot sardines and onions.

Cooked and chopped fish fingers with salted peanuts.

Fried mashed potato, curry powder and 1 teaspoon olive oil blended.

or

Fill the uncooked boat with:

Chopped spring onions or chives and cream cheese.

A mixture of tuna, chopped salted peanuts and shredded onion.

Blended red salmon, chopped spring onions, 1 teaspoon vinegar and paprika.

Grated cheese and sweet pickle.

Cold cooked rice, ½ teaspoon olive oil, 1 clove crushed garlic and curry powder to taste.

Fried tomato, basil (or pesto), fried onion and cold boiled rice.

Cold fried rice (see page 104)

Peppered Eggs

1 green pepper cored and shredded
2 knobs butter
3 medium onions thinly sliced
1 clove of garlic finely chopped or crushed
1 small can of tomatoes drained
4 rashers streaky bacon chopped
2 eggs
½ cup of milk
fresh herbs such as basil if available
toast or fried bread

Boil peppers in salted water for 3 minutes and drain. Fry bacon
until cooked and put aside. Cook vegetables with herbs slowly
over a low heat for 15 minutes. Pour eggs beaten with milk over
the vegetables and heat till nearly set. Add bacon and heat until
egg mixture is properly set. Eat with toast if you are able to make
it, otherwise with lightly fried bread which can be made
beforehand. If you are using fresh herbs, chop and add them to
the eggs just before cooking.

Plain Omelette

4 eggs
4 teaspoons cold water
salt and pepper
1 knob butter

Beat eggs and water lightly and season. Heat butter in pan until sizzling but not brown. Pour in beaten eggs and after about 5 seconds move edges of setting omelette to centre of pan with a knife, fork or spatula. At the same time, tilt pan quickly in all directions so that uncooked egg runs to edges. Cook further ½ to 1 minute. Remove from heat, fold in half in pan, serve garnished with parsley.

Savoury Omelette Fillings -

To be added to beaten eggs.

Ham and potato

1 tablespoon each of diced lightly fried potato and ham.

Fried Onion

1 tablespoon finely chopped fried onion.

Bacon, Mushroom and Onion

1 tablespoon each of bacon, mushroom and onion, finely chopped and fried.

Leek and mushroom

1 tablespoon each of leek, mushroom and onion, finely chopped and fried.

Cheese

2 heaped tablespoons finely grated Cheddar.

Chive and Watercress

2 level tablespoons finely chopped chives, 1 level tablespoon finely chopped watercress.

Filled Omelettes

Cover half the omelette with filling while still in the pan and fold over:

Asparagus

Drained tinned asparagus tips warmed in butter.

Bacon

4-6 rashers, chopped and fried.

Crouton

3 rounded tablespoons golden fried bread cubes.

Chicken

Mug of diced cooked chicken.

Tomato

4 skinned chopped and fried tomatoes

Ham

2 slices ham chopped

Kidney

½ mug thinly sliced fried kidneys.

Mushroom

½ mug thinly sliced, fried mushrooms.

Onion

½ mug sliced fried onions.

Pork and Cheese Grill

2 thick lean pork chops
4 cloves garlic crushed
2 tablespoons olive oil
4 tablespoons chopped salted peanuts
enough cheese slices to cover the chops
fresh basil if available
salt and pepper
Worcestershire sauce

Brush chops with oil, add garlic and sprinkle with salt and pepper.
Grill for about 7 minutes a side until juices run clear when
pierced.Cover the chops with slices of cheese, sprinkle with nuts
and cook until cheese melts. Add a dash of Worcestershire sauce
and sprinkle again with nuts.

Pork Belly Kebabs

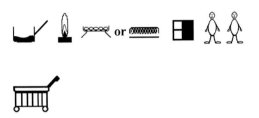

4 strips of pork belly cubed
1 small can pineapple cubes
2 tablespoons vinegar
1 red pepper and 1 green pepper cut into squares
10 or so button mushrooms
oil
1 tablespoon tomato purée
2 tablespoons Worcestershire sauce
1 tablespoon soy sauce
2 tablespoons brown sugar
¼ teaspoon chilli powder
2 teaspoons cornflour
salt and pepper

Thread meat, pineapple and vegetables alternately onto skewers.
Mix purée, vinegar, sugar, sauces, chilli, salt and pepper with the
pineapple juice and heat to boiling. Mix the cornflour with a little
cold water and stir into hot sauce. Heat for a further minute or
two and brush on the kebabs. Grill for about ten minutes, turning
and brushing frequently with the sauce.

Pork Stir Fry

2 slices of pork belly or a medium sized piece of tenderloin cut
into bite sized pieces
1 tablespoon oil
1 large onion chopped
1 red pepper chopped
1 stick of celery chopped
2 or 3 mushrooms chopped
1 carrot chopped
a handful of bean sprouts
plum sauce and soy sauce to taste
cornflour

Fry the pork and when cooked add the chopped vegetables to the
pan over a high flame for a few minutes. Add the bean sprouts
with the plum sauce and soy sauce. Mix a little cornflour with cold
water and add to the pan. Cook until the sauce thickens and add
more water if necessary. Serve with rice or Chinese noodles.

Quick Cream Sauce

For veal, poultry, egg and cheese dishes:

1 can condensed cream soup
4 tablespoons fresh cream or milk

Heat and stir gently together. Pour over food or serve separately

Variously flavoured soups may be used, depending on preference and the type of dish with which it is to be used. Packet soups can also be used but the quantity of water may need to be reduced or the liquid reduced by boiling off before adding the cream or milk.

Quick Grilled Steak

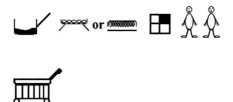

2 medium onions chopped
2 thick quick fry steaks

Sauce ingredients:

3 tablespoons ketchup
1 tablespoon soy sauce
1 teaspoon mustard powder
1 teaspoon brown sugar
1 tablespoon Worcestershire sauce
1 tablespoon wine, cider or malt vinegar
¼ teaspoon paprika

Mix all the sauce ingredients. Season steaks and brush with oil.
Seal both sides of steak over hot coals or under preheated grill for
a minute. Coat with sauce mixture and grill each side for another
4-5 minutes or until done to taste. Brush frequently with mixture.
Eat with salad or jacket potatoes or both.

Red Cabbage Salad

1 piece red cabbage shredded
1 medium onion finely sliced
1 large carrot shredded
2 tablespoons cider or wine vinegar
1 teaspoon honey
1 tablespoon olive oil
1 tablespoon sesame seeds
3 tablespoons grated Parmesan cheese
1 tablespoon crushed salted peanuts or similar

Blend the vinegar, honey, oil, Parmesan and nuts. Pour over the salad vegetables and mix well. Sprinkle with sesame seeds. White cabbage can be used if preferred.

Rice and Mixed Vegetable Salad

1 mug cold boiled rice
1 mug radishes topped and tailed
6-8 spring onions chopped
a handful of roasted salted peanuts
1 small bunch watercress chopped
1 tablespoon soy sauce

Cook rice and rinse well with cold water. Drain. Mix all
ingredients thoroughly.

"Give an old guy enough rope ..."

Risotto

2 knobs butter
1 onion finely chopped
2 dozen or so button mushrooms thinly sliced
1 cup dry white wine
1½ mugs long grain rice
1½ mugs meat or vegetable stock (Oxo or similar cubes in hot water)
1 mug grated Parmesan cheese

Cook onion in half the butter over low heat until soft and transparent. Add mushrooms and stir gently. Add wine and stir over heat until evaporated. Add rice and cook gently for a minute and then add half the stock, cooking and stirring until absorbed. Add more stock in small quantities until absorbed each time. After 20 minutes, the rice should be cooked and tender, but with each grain still keeping its shape. Season to taste, add rest of butter and Parmesan. Let stand for 3 minutes. Serve with watercress, celery and spring onion salad.

Roast Garlic Parsnips

2 medium parsnips
aluminium foil
2 cloves garlic sliced
dark soy sauce
cheese

Cut small slits in the parsnips and insert slivers of garlic. Wrap in foil and seal well. Bake on embers or under grill until cooked. Open top of foil and put a slice of Cheddar cheese on the parsnips. Heat until cheese melts and sprinkle with soy sauce.

Serve with grilled meat or fish.

This recipe can be used for leeks, carrots or whole smallish onions.

You can also foil wrap the Pepper and Cheese Boats on page 57 for the whole of the cooking time if more convenient.

Salad Dressings

1 Mix 2 teaspoons each of orange juice, prepared pesto and olive oil with 1 teaspoon each of ground coriander, mustard powder, white wine vinegar and black pepper. Add a pinch of salt and stir well just before pouring on salad. This is also delicious with barbecued lamb chops.

2 Mix 4 teaspoons each of soy sauce, white wine vinegar, Worcestershire sauce and brown sugar with 2 tablepoons of olive oil and 1 teaspoon ground cumin.

3 Mix 2 teaspoons brown sugar and 1 teaspoon ground ginger with 4 teaspoons lemon juice. This can also be used with grilled meat or fish as a sauce.For the salad dressing, add 4 teaspoons olive oil if wished.

4 Mix 4 tablespoons mayonnaise with ½ teaspoon black pepper, 1 teaspoon cumin and 1 teaspoon ground coriander.

5 Mix 4 tablespoons plain yogourt, a wedge of blue cheese crumbled, 2 table spoons orange juice, ½ teaspoon black pepper, 1 teaspoon ground ginger, 2 teaspoons brown sugar and 2 tablespoons olive oil.

6 Mix 6 tablespoons single cream with 1 teaspoon ground cumin, 1 teaspoon lemon juice, ½ teaspoon black pepper, ½ teaspoon salt and 1 teaspoon sugar.

7 Mix 4 teaspoons olive oil with 4 teaspoons balsamic vinegar and a teaspoon of Dijon mustard. Add salt and pepper to taste.

8 A handful of blackberries, boiled with a little water until cooked - about 3 minutes. Beat or shake together in a jar with 3 tablespoons of corn oil, 2 tablespoons olive oil, salt and pepper to taste.

Salade Niçoise

4 or 5 fairly large potatoes
4 eggs
1 pack French beans
3 tomatoes
2 Little Gem lettuces or similar
1 can anchovies in olive oil, drained
12 pitted black olives
1 large can tuna in olive oil
8 tablespoons ready-made French dressing or use a salad dressing
from page 72

Cut potatoes into even cubes and cook in salted water until tender.
Drain and cool. Hard boil (5-8 minutes) the eggs. Drain, cool, shell
and chop into quarters. Cook beans in salted water for 8-10
minutes. Drain, rinse in cold water and chop into short lengths.
Cut tomatoes into wedges. Drain and flake the tuna. Gently mix
with all the ingredients in a bowl and pour 2 tablespoons of
dressing over each portion.

Sausage Kebabs

1 red pepper and 1 green pepper deseeded and cut into squares
1 large onion peeled and cut into segments
1 mango or papaya peeled and diced
3-4 tablespoons olive oil
1 clove garlic crushed
8 herb sausages halved
4 kebab skewers
salt and pepper

Thread alternately the sausage and other ingredients on the
skewers which have been previously soaked in water to prevent
burning if they are wooden. Mix oil, garlic and seasoning and
brush on vegetables. Grill or barbecue for 3-6 minutes each side,
recoating frequently with dressing. Serve with boiled rice (started
cooking before the kebab) and a simple green salad of say, lettuce
and cucumber.

Sausage Salad

4 mugs of pasta twists or similar
4 low fat sausages grilled and thinly sliced
1 red pepper seeded and sliced
4 spring onions chopped
4 tablespoons mayonnaise
3 tablespoons Greek style yogourt
3 tablespoons freshly chopped coriander
sprig of parsley
salt and pepper

Cook pasta in boiling salted water for about 10-12 minutes, drain and rinse in cold water. Drain again and put aside. Grill, barbecue or fry sausages according to means available and allow to cool. Mix chopped sausages with pasta, red pepper and spring onions. Beat together dressing ingredients and mix well with pasta and sausage. Season and garnish with parsley. Cool if you have the means before serving.

Savoury Baguette

2 knobs butter / tablespoons oil
1 medium onion
6 medium mushrooms
4 rashers bacon / slices of salami / garlic or similar sausage
1 baguette, either stale or fresh, salt and pepper

Put half the oil / butter in the pan to heat. Fry on the flat side the bread which has been cut into pan-sized slices, cooking until golden. Put aside, then roughly chop the meat and vegetables and cook until tender - about 5 minutes. Season to taste. Use the cooked vegetable and meat mixture as a hot sandwich filling. If the bread is fresh, there is no need to fry - toast it.

" Guys and Hols - sweet music!"

Savoury Leek Nests

2 large potatoes
1 large leek sliced lengthways
1 large onion sliced
6 large mushrooms chopped
2 eggs
2 tablespoons oil
1 clove garlic crushed

Cut potatoes into small cubes and boil with leeks until cooked. Fry onions and mushrooms until just soft. Remove leeks and drain separately. Drain and mash potatoes. Mix onions, garlic and mushrooms with potato and place two mounds in the pan in a little hot oil. Hollow out the mound but do not remove any of the mixture; pile it around the centre so that the pan surface is exposed. Crack an egg into each and arrange the leeks around the outside. Cook until the eggs are set.

Sherried Mushrooms

a handful of open cup mushrooms quartered
1 onion chopped
2 knobs butter
¼ teaspoon ground mace
2 tablespoons flour
1 mug chicken or vegetarian stock
4 tablespoons sherry or similar
1 tablespoon tomato paste
salt and pepper

Fry mushrooms and onions in butter for 2-3 minutes. Stir in mace and flour. Remove from heat, Slowly add stock and return to heat. Bring back to boil. Add sherry, tomato paste, salt and pepper and simmer for 2 minutes. Serve hot or cold with fish, meat or vegetable dishes.

Smoked Mackerel and Potato Salad

1 can of new potatoes
1 can of hot (ie peppered) smoked mackerel fillets
a few spring onions finely chopped
3 tablespoons mayonnaise
2 carrots grated
1 teaspoon lemon juice
Salt and pepper

Heat can of potatoes as per instructions on label, leaving to keep warm in liquid. Mix remaining ingredients, drain potatoes and add. Season to taste.

"I'm inclined to give a guy a chance"

Spaghetti Bolognese

1 onion finely chopped
2 knobs butter
enough minced beef for 4 people
6 or so mushrooms chopped
1 mug water
1 can tomato paste
2 teaspoons sugar
1 teaspoon basil or mixed herbs
1 bay leaf if available
1 clove garlic chopped
salt and pepper
spaghetti sufficient for four people
About 1 mug grated Cheddar or Parmesan as an accompaniment

Fry onion slowly until pale gold, add beef and break up. Continue cooking for further 3 or 4 minutes, stirring continuously. Add rest of ingredients apart from spaghetti and cheese. Season. Bring slowly to boil, stirring. Cover and lower heat. Simmer for 30 minutes until half the liquid has evaporated. Meanwhile cook spaghetti in boiling salted water for about 20 minutes. Drain and pour sauce over pasta. Sprinkle with cheese.

Spanish Omelette

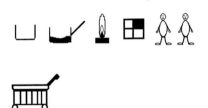

1 cored and chopped green pepper
2 knobs butter
4 or 5 medium potatoes peeled and diced
4 eggs
4 tablespoons milk
½ cup of grated hard cheese
1 large chopped onion
salt and pepper
herbs if available - parsley, oregano, basil etc.

Boil chopped pepper for 5 minutes in salted water and drain. Fry onion and potatoes very slowly in butter until almost cooked through. Beat eggs and milk with fork, seasoning to taste. Raise heat and add green pepper, continuing to cook until vegetables start to brown. Pour over egg mixture, stirring once or twice. Leave in pan until omelette starts to set and the underside is beginning to brown. Scatter grated cheese over omelette and turn. After a few moments, cut, sprinkle with fresh herbs and serve.

Spiced Kidney Beans

1 large can kidney beans
1 mug water
2 crushed cloves garlic
½ teaspoon ginger
1 teaspoon turmeric
1 teaspoon chilli powder
1 teaspoon garam masala
1 large knob of butter

Fry the garlic, chilli powder, ginger and turmeric for a few
moments in the butter. Rinse the kidney beans, add to the pan with
the water. Bring to the boil, reduce to simmer and cook until the
sauce thickens. Add the garam masala and cook for a few
moments more. Serve hot.

Spicy Sausage Hotpot

1 pack of sausages
1 tablespoon olive oil
1 onion sliced
1 red pepper thinly sliced
1 yellow pepper thinly sliced
2 cloves garlic crushed
2 teaspoons fennel seeds
2 teaspoons paprika
1 can of chopped tomatoes
1 chicken stock cube in a mug of hot water

Fry sausages until cooked. Remove from pan and set aside. Fry onions and peppers until soft. Stir in remaining ingredients and season to taste. Bring to boil, reduce heat and simmer for 15 minutes. Stir occasionally until sauce is thickened. Slice sausages into bite sized pieces and add. Simmer for further 10 minutes.

Meanwhile cook pasta - fusilli, spaghetti etc as desired. Garnish with chopped oregano and grated Parmesan cheese.

Stuffed Chicken Breasts

a handful of oyster mushrooms
4 boneless chicken breasts
1 clove garlic crushed
a mug of orange juice
1 onion diced
4 tablespoons breadcrumbs
1 egg beaten
4 tablespoons walnuts chopped
2 teaspoons mixed herbs
4 knobs butter
small pot cream
a few cocktail sticks
parsley for garnish

Mix mushrooms, garlic, onion, orange juice, breadcrumbs, egg, walnuts and herbs in a bowl. Flatten breasts or slit carefully lengthwise. Place stuffing on or in the breasts and "sew" together with cocktail sticks. Melt butter in pan, add a little orange juice then fry stuffed breasts over medium heat. Remove breasts, stir in cream until sauce thickens a little. Spoon sauce over breasts and serve garnished with parsley.

Sweet Corn and Anchovy Salad

1 can anchovy fillets drained
1 can sweet corn drained
8 spring onions chopped
2 tablespoons plain yogourt
4 tablespoons fromage frais
1 red pepper sliced
2 cloves garlic crushed
1 teaspoon cumin
1 teaspoon lemon juice
2 medium potatoes diced and cooked
pepper to taste

Mix all ingredients thoroughly.

Sweet and Sour Chicken

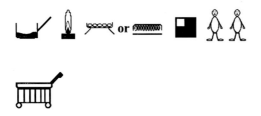

2 chicken pieces
1 small can crushed pineapple
1 small can tomatoes
3 tablespoons sugar
4 tablespoons vinegar
3 tablespoons soy sauce
2 tablespoons cornflour
1 mug water
salt and pepper
rice for 2 people

Brush chicken with oil and put to grill or barbecue. Heat sugar,
vinegar and soy sauce in a pan. Blend cornflour and a little water
in a cup or similar until smooth. Add cornflour mixture to pan and
stir until blended and thick. Simmer for 5 minutes. Add pineapple,
tomatoes, seasoning and rest of water. Then add the thoroughly
cooked chicken and simmer for 10 minutes over low heat. Eat
with boiled rice.

Sweet and Sour Pork

2 pieces belly of pork cut into bite sized pieces
1 tablespoon oil
1 large onion sliced
1 green pepper sliced
1 carrot sliced
1 small can pineapple chunks
2 tablespoons tomato paste
1 tablespoon vinegar
1 tablespoon soy sauce
brown sugar to taste
cornflour

Fry pork in oil until slightly browned, add the sliced vegetables and cook on a high flame for a few minutes. Add pineapple chunks and some of the juice together with the tomato paste, vinegar and soy sauce, and sugar to taste. Mix a little cornflour with cold water and add to pan, cooking until mixture thickens. Serve with boiled rice.

Sweet and Sour Sauce

2 knobs of butter
2 medium onions finely chopped
2 rashers of bacon
2 tablespoons tomato paste
1 mug cider
½ mug water
1 tablespoon sugar
2 tablespoons Worcestershire sauce
2 tablespoons mango chutney
3 teaspoons cornflour
salt and pepper to taste

Fry onions and bacon in the oil and butter until soft. Add all other ingredients except cornflour. Bring to boil, then simmer for 15-20 minutes. Blend cornflour with little water, add to the pan and cook for one minute, stirring all the time. Serve hot or cold with meat or poultry.

Tagliatelle, Bacon and Pesto

1 tablespoon olive oil
2 cloves garlic crushed
2 heaped tablespoons Parmesan cheese
a few olives
12 rashers unsmoked rindless bacon cut into strips
tagliatelle sufficient for two (see pack)
small carton double cream
pesto

Heat oil, add garlic and bacon. Cook over medium heat for 5-6 minutes, stirring occasionally. Meanwhile put pasta into boiling water and cook for time given on pack. Drain and add to bacon mixture, stir in cream, pesto, cheese and seasoning to taste. Cook for a couple of minutes and garnish with basil and olives before serving.

Thick Onion Soup

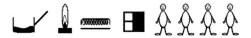

4 - 6 large onions thinly sliced
2 knobs of butter
3 mugs beef stock
4 slices of French bread
½ mug of grated cheese (Cheddar or similar)
Worcestershire sauce
2 tablespoons light soy sauce
2 tablespoons Parmesan cheese
2 tablespoons flour
salt and pepper to taste

Fry onions in butter in a saucepan until golden. Add flour and stir over heat for a couple of minutes. Add stock and sauce, stirring well. Season to taste. Bring to boil, add grated cheeses, cover pan and simmer for 20 minutes. Grill Cheddar on the slices of bread and float on the soup as served. Chunks of Cheddar cheese can be added to the boiling soup during the last ten minutes.

Tomato and Yogourt Salad

1 large carton natural yogourt
2 tablespoons pesto
6-8 medium tomatoes chopped
1 dozen or so spring onions chopped
a handful of salted roast peanuts
seasoning

Season and mix all ingredients.

Trout with Nuts

4 trout
2 knobs butter melted
seasoning
lemon juice
4 tablespoons salted roast peanuts or almonds
1 knob of butter rolled into 4 balls
mixed herbs

Cut 4 pieces of aluminium foil large enough for each fish and
brush foil and fish generously with melted butter. Pierce several
holes to allow drainage. Sprinkle fish with lemon juice, seasoning
and herbs and parcel up. Grill or barbecue for about 15 minutes or
longer according to size. When done, add a butterball to each,
sprinkled with crushed nuts. Potato chips can be made in a similar
way by wrapping in foil with butter and grilling or barbecuing. The
packets can be opened for the last few minutes cooking time.

Turkey in Paprika

1 large onion chopped
1 small red pepper chopped
2 knobs butter
2 teaspoons oil
1 tablespoon flour
1-2 teaspoons paprika
1 teaspoon tomato paste
1 teaspoon sugar
1 mug stock
½ teaspoon salt
½ teaspoon caraway seeds
4 cooked turkey steaks
1 small carton yogourt

Fry onion and pepper in oil and butter until soft and golden.
Remove from heat and stir in flour, paprika, tomato paste and
sugar. Blend in stock, salt and caraway seeds. Cook and stir until
mixture comes to boil and thickens. Cover and simmer for 15
minutes. Chop turkey and add with yogourt to pan. Heat through
for 5 minutes without boiling. Eat with potatoes, rice, noodles or
pasta.

Turkish Pilaff

2-3 tablespoons olive oil
2 small onions finely chopped
1 large tomato skinned seeded and chopped
1 green or red pepper finely chopped
1 mug short grained rice
2 mugs chicken or vegetarian stock (stock cube in water)
salt and black pepper

Fry the onions, tomato and pepper until just soft. Add rice and fry until transparent. Stir spoonsful of stock into the mixture and simmer until all the liquid has been absorbed by the rice and the latter is cooked - about 15-20 minutes.

Veal Patties

4 slices bread (crusts removed)
milk
1 large onion finely chopped
pack of minced veal (or beef)
salt and pepper
2 knobs butter
a handful of mushrooms sliced
2 heaped tablespoons flour
1 can tomatoes
1 tablespoon lemon juice
1 stock cube
1 mug water
1 teaspoon sugar
1 teaspoon tomato paste
3 tablespoons soured cream, chopped parsley

Put bread into dish and just cover with milk. Mix onions with meat, seasoning with salt and pepper. Squeeze bread and fork into meat. Knead and divide into 12. Roll into balls and then flatten. Sprinkle both sides with flour and fry in butter until done. Remove from pan. Fry mushrooms with remaining butter and put with meat patties. Add to the buttery juices in the pan, flour, tomatoes, lemon juice, stock cube, water, tomato paste, salt and pepper. Whisk over medium heat until sauce thickens. Add patties and mushrooms and heat over low flame for a few more minutes. Before serving, pour soured cream over and sprinkle with parsley. Serve with a green salad.

Vegetable Bites

 Heat salted peanuts on barbecue in metal dish, saucepan or mess tin. Sprinkle with a mixture of soy sauce, crushed garlic and curry powder.

 Deep fried mushrooms with garlic butter and plenty of French bread.

 Fried bread with fried chopped mushrooms, onion and bacon with a dash of soy sauce.

 Heat salted peanuts in metal dish, add grated Cheddar and continue heating until cheese is melted.

 Grill mushrooms with olive oil and then add grated cheese. Grill until cheese is melted.

Vegetable Curry

mixed chopped vegetables, according to taste, and sufficient
quantity for four people
1 onion chopped
1 knob margarine
2 tablespoons curry powder
1 chicken or vegetarian stock cube in 2 mugs of water
1 tablespoon plain flour
1 tablespoon mango chutney
salt and pepper

Fry the onion and curry powder in the margarine for 2 or 3
minutes. Add the remaining vegetables with the flour and cook for
a further 3 minutes, stirring. Add the stock and mango chutney to
the pan, bring to the boil and simmer for 30 minutes or so. Serve
with rice.

Viennese Sausage with Eggs

4 slices streaky bacon
2 pork sausages
3 eggs
4 tablespooons milk
1 large knob butter or margarine
salt and pepper

Lightly fry the sausages and cut into pieces, add the chopped
bacon to the pan and cook together for a further 5 minutes.
Beat the eggs, milk and salt and pepper in a bowl and add to the
saucepan. Stir over a reduced heat until thick and lightly
scrambled. Eat with crusty bread.

West Coast Bean Jar

2 slices of belly of pork chopped
1 onion chopped
1 stock cube
1 can Pinto or Black Eyed beans
oil
salt and pepper

Fry the belly of pork until brown, add the onion and continue to fry until cooked. Put the drained tinned beans into the pot with sufficient water to cover. Break up the stock cube and add with salt and pepper to taste. Simmer until thoroughly heated through and the fluid is reduced by about half.

Western Beans

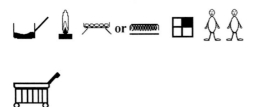

1 tablespoon oil
1 medium onion chopped
2 rashers bacon chopped
1 teaspoon Worcestershire sauce
2 teaspoons mustard
1 can baked beans
1 pack sausages
1 level teaspoon black pepper

Fry onion and bacon, add rest of ingredients and heat through.
Serve with grilled or barbecued sausages.

"Guys get around me easily" says Peg

Wet Weather Stew

1 small swede
1 medium parsnip
1 large onion
1 turnip
6 large mushrooms
1 stick of celery
2 stock cubes
1 red pepper
2 tablespoons flour
salt and pepper
4 pieces of stewing steak
4 potatoes
4 tablespoons oil
mixed herbs

Dice and fry the steak in a large saucepan for 3-4 minutes. Add chopped vegetables and continue to fry, turning frequently for another 3-4 minutes. Add flour and stir well. Mix stock cubes in a mug of warm water and pour into pan, stirring well. Continue to cook for a few minutes, add seasoning to taste, then cover and simmer for ¾ hour until meat is tender. Fresh herbs can be added a few minutes before serving if they are available.

Worcester Beef Kebabs

large piece rump steak cubed
3 tablespoons clear honey
1 tablespoon soy sauce
2 tablespoons plum sauce or marmalade
1 tablespoon Worcester sauce
1 tablespoon sesame seeds
1 teaspoon Chinese Five Spice powder
8 wooden skewers soaked in water to prevent them from burning

Mix all ingredients apart from steak to make marinade. Add meat,
cover and leave for as long as possible to marinate (3-4 hours if
possible). Boil remaining marinade until it is thick enough to form
a glaze. Thread meat onto skewers and brush with glaze.
Barbecue or grill for 6-8 minutes, turning occasionally and
brushing with glaze. Serve with salad and pitta bread or crisp rolls.

Yachtsman's Lamb Chops

4 lamb chops
1 teaspoon paprika
1 large onion, chopped
1 can tomatoes, chopped
1 teaspoon mixed herbs
oil for frying
salt and pepper

Mix the paprika, salt and pepper and rub into the chops. Fry in the oil until cooked, remove from the pan and keep hot. Fry the chopped onion in the same pan until tender and add the tomatoes and mixed herbs. Cook for an additional 3 or 4 minutes. Return the chops to the pan for a further few minutes. Serve with potatoes or rice, or eat with fresh bread.

Yangtze Fried Rice

1 onion finely chopped
2 mushrooms finely chopped
1 red, yellow or green pepper finely chopped
2 eggs
1 mug of rice
oil

Cook rice in boiling water until just soft, drain and rinse with cold water. Fry vegetables gently until soft and add rice. Fry vegetables and rice until thoroughly warmed through. Beat eggs and dribble into hot mixture, stirring continuously. Fry for a few moments after all the egg has set and serve.

Yeoman's Pork Chops

2 pork chops
a handful of blackberries - an August camping treat!
1 teaspoon honey
1 clove garlic, crushed
salt and pepper
oil

Grill, barbecue or fry the chops. In the mean time stew the blackberries in very little water, adding the honey, garlic and salt and pepper to taste. Pour over the chops.

Movable Bean Feasts

ISBN 0 9533386 2 2

The companion volume to *Movable Feasts,* but this time **for vegetarians.**

Again, there are over 100 easy but often unusual recipes for people on the move, on holiday or in accommodation where facilities may be limited.

The book is down to earth, practical and fun as you would expect from this no-nonsense author.

Order it from your local bookshop
or direct from the Publishers £6.99 plus postage and packing £1.25

Editions de la
Montagne

PO Box 732
Southampton
SO16 7RQ
England

From the same Publisher:

Camping and Caravanning in France
The "Survival" Guide
by Rick Allen

ISBN   0 9533386 0 6

The Guide for the motorist, biker, backpacker, cyclist, camper, caravanner and motorcaravanner or the ordinary traveller in France, French speaker or not

Price £9.99 including postage to purchasers of
Movable Feasts or *Movable Bean Feasts*

Offer applicable only to mail order purchases direct from the Publisher

Editions de la Montagne
PO Box 732
Southampton
SO16 7RQ
UK

Bookshop price normally £12.50

If you have enjoyed using this recipe book, why not send in your own recipes for inclusion in our next book:

Please send your ideas to the Publisher:

Editions de la Montagne
PO Box 732
Southampton
SO16 7RQ
England

Thank you!

"Anyone need a Peg going spare....!!"

Index

Notes